The CALL *to* CARE

VOLUNTEER TRAINING

LILLIAN M. EASTERLY-SMITH, BCPC

LIFE CARE PUBLISHING

LifeCare Publishing
A ministry of LifeCare Christian Center
33300 Warren Rd., Ste. 17
Westland, MI 48185 USA
www.lifecarechristiancenter.org

Unless otherwise noted, all Scripture quotations are taken from the HOLY BIBLE, NEW INTERNATIONAL VERSION® (NIV). Copyright © 1973, 1978, 1984 International Bible Society. Used by permission of Zondervan. All rights reserved.

Scripture marked (NCV) is taken from the New Century Version. Copyright © 2005 by Thomas Nelson, Inc. Used by permission. All rights reserved.

Images and descriptions for "So You Have a Toothache?" in Section V are used courtesy of Equipping Ministries International from their publication, *Listening for Heaven's Sake* by Gary R. Sweeten, et al., ©1993 by Teleios Publications, a division of Equipping Ministries International, Inc., Cincinnati, Ohio. The Alternate "Dead Dog" Scenario in the Appendix is also used courtesy of Equipping Ministries International.

Special thanks for Music for the Soul **www.musicforthesoul.org** for the use of their music Binder of the Broken in the DVD menu.

Printed & Manufactured in the United States of America

ISBN: 978-0615836362

CONTENTS

ACKNOWLEDGMENTS

*T*hank you, Lord Jesus, for teaching me how to live and love. It is through my life lessons and all that you have taught me that I am able to pass on what is in these pages. If it were not for your intervention in my life, I am certain that I would not be here today. Thank you for the many people in Alcoholics for Christ that you used to bring healing to my soul, and those who inspired and encouraged me to step out in faith and use the gifts you have given me.

Thank you to my LifeCare family—those who put in tireless hours to make this ministry happen, as well as those who come to get help and support—I learn from you on a regular basis and am blessed beyond measure! Many thanks to the Board of Directors— each one of you dreams big God-dreams with me and you're willing to take risks to make the dreams happen. Special thanks to Patti, who serves on the board and co-facilitated this training—you are outstanding; and to Kelly—the editing, planning and preparation, WOW—you served tirelessly in this endeavor. I am still amazed by your talents and stamina. Thank you.

I cannot say enough about Pastor Mike Morche and his wonderful team of volunteers who blessed us not only with the facility to film, but helped us with staging and many other details that made the environment set for production—God bless you! Natalie and Valeria, great photos—thank you for blessing us with your expertise!

Thank you to our drama team who made the sketch in this training come to life (with humor) —Mike, Gracie, Joyce, Carol, you are a joy! And to those who willingly participated and made the entire time much more interesting because of the interaction, thank you—may God bless you for your time and belief in this project. To Siege Media, again, what professionalism in your filming and preparation. I am still amazed by your talent, but more than that, I love your hearts, Jake and Jacque. And Don, you were right on top of the tech and sound—thank you for being there and believing in what we do. Maureen, the words "thank you" do not seem to be enough—you have given many hours to this cause, we could not do it without you!

Thank you to my family who believed in and supported me as I struggled through my own challenges to get to a place of healing and on to investing my time, talents and gifts to make a difference in people's lives. And to my husband, Mike, my partner for life and partner in ministry, I know your heart beats the same desire as mine, to see people be set free and enjoy the life God has designed for them. I can honestly say that there is no one on earth I would rather share this with than YOU! Thank you for sharing me with others and being available to use your gifts in this ministry. You are the best!

WELCOME

$\mathcal{W}$elcome to LifeCare's Volunteer Training. The goal of the training is to provide an awareness of LifeCare's purpose, values and leadership expectations as well as some practical facilitation skills.

The following pages are a mixture of knowledge and experience gained from many thought-out plans and even mistakes over the course of my 21-year journey in developing ministries that provide care, support and healing. My God-given passion is to see these types of ministries exist around the world in every church or made available to people in congregations through a para-church organization strategically placed in communities to offer help and hope. If you are reading this text and watching the DVD training made available to you, I know you must have the same desire and passion. Perhaps you, like me, have learned the need for a ministry like this from your own personal journey and need.

Your involvement in Care & Support Ministries in your church and community will enable you to take others by the hand and lead them down the path of healing that God designs for each of them. God never wastes a hurt, so your past hurts and experiences will now be used to bring healing to others and glory to God. I believe that many things individuals deal with in life (struggles, hurts, addictions) will not be fully healed apart from the involvement of others—relationship. The more I do this ministry, the more I see that this is absolutely part of God's plan and design. We were made for relationship—deep, intimate, trusting relationship. At support groups, in particular, we see this happening on a regular basis, and that is why I am excited for you—excited that you have made the decision to get involved, be trained and take the risk God is asking of you. Trust me, you will never regret it. It is not easy by any means—dealing with people is messy; however, it is the most rewarding experience, I believe, you could ever have. May God bless you, strengthen you, and give you wisdom as He equips you to do His work.

WHO WE ARE

*L*ifeCare Christian Center is a nonprofit, inter-denominational organization in the service of providing individuals and families in the community with physical, spiritual, emotional and relational support while walking through life's challenges. It is a safe place where people can share and support one another.

Those who offer care and assistance help the attendees through the process of healing and growth by becoming open and transparent with God, themselves and others. This process allows individuals the opportunity to change from the inside out—overcoming mistrust, anger, addictions, hurt, rejection, compulsions, unforgiveness and other issues of the heart. In return, they will receive peace, serenity, joy and most importantly, a stronger relationship with God and others.

LifeCare, through its community enrichment programs, endeavors to recruit and develop pastors, staff and lay volunteers in care-giving skills and to train them using the most up-to-date and comprehensive curriculums, along with the expertise of area professionals, pastors and experienced lay people. All of LifeCare's volunteers have life experience as well as training from some of the best professionals and courses available in the nation.

WHAT OTHERS ARE SAYING ABOUT LIFECARE

"When I first came to LifeCare, I looked at the classes that were offered. Thinking <u>carefully</u> about what help I needed, I slowly rose my hand with the pencil in it and closed my eyes. Keeping my eyes closed, I lowered the pencil down to the list. I opened my eyes to see my destiny. It didn't really matter because I knew I had to start somewhere, and there wasn't a class offered that I didn't need....

"Now, I know who I am in God and on Earth. I don't need a man to make me whole, I have let go of the anger I have had against my parents as well as those who have wronged me, and I have learned to forgive them. I have learned to honestly pray for my enemies. I have learned to respect others' boundaries as well as practice my own without feeling bad about myself. Most importantly, I have learned to let God forgive me and then forgive myself.

"I have also learned to use my life experiences to help others. I facilitate the DivorceCare® class and it is such a joy to see healing going on and know that it is all in God's plan. I feel so blessed to be used in serving Him. As I served this past year, I was blessed even more. I was holding on to something that I hadn't realized, and in my leading this class, God released this hurt from my heart. What joy I experienced having this burden lifted. LifeCare has led me to a new life, freeing me and filling me with love and hope, replacing the doom and gloom that was my life in the past."

—*Joyce, LifeCare participant and group leader*

"I came initially to just 'learn' about LifeCare and inner healing prayer. Next thing I knew, I realized I needed healing and started regular sessions with a facilitator to get those wounds from my past addressed. I knew I didn't want to live under that bondage anymore; it was time to get rid of it and walk in the fullness of Christ and the freedom only He can bring.

"Before long, I had grown into a woman with confidence. I was very serious about inner healing prayer and learned as much as I could about it. The LORD was showing up in unbelievable ways during my sessions and I was moving into more peace each time. I grew to know HIS voice, HIS way of communicating with me like never before! I understood HIM at a completely different level.

"The next thing I knew, Lillian encouraged me to move into a position of facilitating a training class. The confidence she had in me was more than anyone had ever shown me. Lillian knows how to pull your gifts out and knows how to set you in your position to do what GOD is calling you into. She has wonderful discernment and a great gift for leading. If it wasn't for her and LifeCare, I wouldn't be where I am today. I am still growing, seeking and running after GOD…but now with joy and confidence because I know deep in my spirit, HE is running after me too!"
—Annamarie, LifeCare volunteer

"I have been involved in Care ministries for approximately 9 years. At first I was in a group called Hopekeepers. It was a group for people dealing with chronic illness. I struggled with Lupus. I learned that even if my body was disabled, my spirit wasn't.

"After meeting with a counselor, she recommended I take the class Boundaries. I had been in an emotionally abusive marriage for 32 years. I was dealing with a passive aggressive man and the stress of the marriage was wreaking havoc on my health. Every few years I would have a lupus flare-up because of what was happening in the marriage. I learned it was okay to draw the line in the sand and say no more.

"When I would talk to him about what was going on, he would just stop talking to me and the children, not answer the phone, not answer the door. These pouts would last 1 or 2 weeks, one time he kept it up for a month. Later I realized this was his way to control me.

"I was strengthened and supported through the care ministries and the counselor that helped me to see what I was really dealing with.

"I believe our lives are our training ground. Because of the life I've lived, I am able to come alongside other women who are struggling with boundaries and even abuse. I have learned how much God hates abuse.

"LifeCare is a place you can be safe, learn the tools for life, and with our Lord's help, we can all handle anything together. You don't have to go through whatever it is you are struggling with alone. In LifeCare you will find the support you need, and along with Jesus' love and care, help to handle your life."
—*D. A., LifeCare participant and volunteer*

"LifeCare helped me overcome my own wounds from the past by providing a safe place to share my struggles and receive the grace and support I needed to grow in my faith. My trust in Christ grew as I experienced the love and support from others who understood my pain. LifeCare also gave me the skills and confidence I needed to effectively help others dealing with emotional pain and anger. Today I have the opportunity and privilege to help women struggling with hurts from the past as well as the current pain of unemployment in this difficult economy.

"LifeCare has also helped to equip me as I'm working to build a care ministry for college students in my church. If every church embraced this type of ministry, and every believer seriously participated, there would be no shortage of leaders, volunteers or finances to achieve the church's mission."
—*Marie, LifeCare participant and group leader*

"LifeCare partnering with our church was and is one of the biggest gifts God has ever given to us. You don't know what you are missing until

God sends something so valuable and says, 'This is what My church as a whole needs!'

"To have counseling and support and recovery groups meeting on our campus without the financial obligation that hiring dozens of counseling Pastors would require is too good for words.

"Every church should seek a LifeCare Ministry for their people and their community. It truly reaches across lines and barriers that keep people separated."
—*Sonny Hennessy, Executive Pastor, Real Life Church, Plymouth, MI*

"I'm a member of the Healing Tears group. I'm amazed, each and every week, to realize that I am not the only one going through the gamut of emotions and feelings I experience. Sometimes I feel so alone, then I read my workbook and I feel like I could have written the exact sentences I'm reading! I get to the group on Thursday night and find that other women have answered the questions almost exactly the same way I did. I am not alone! I thank God for the support I get from LifeCare. My prayer is that someday the healing tears I'm shedding right now will be my gateway to being able to help others. Thank you LifeCare! Thank you Lillian! Thank you Kelly and my friends in Healing Tears!"
—*Maureen, LifeCare group participant and volunteer*

"There was a time in my life when I was chronically relapsing. I would go out and use a substance ONCE, not a binge or months/ years relapse, but just once, but had to come back and admit my slip/ relapse to my fellow AA groups with great shame. I kept telling myself this would be the last time…it never was. I was going to a counselor who told me about a church, and I later found out about a help ministry from the Pastor of that church. Within days I was hooked up with Lillian and then another counselor, Pam. I worked with Pam for a long time, and during that time, she and Lillian said rehab was a necessity for me. I didn't want to go, but when I passed out IN the church passing out programs, it was a sign. I went to Brighton, came back and had ANOTHER relapse. I thought I knew

God was with me through all this...but never saw/ felt him. It wasn't until I had to go admit to Lillian that I relapsed AGAIN!!!! When she looked at me and said that we need to work on what is causing the chronic relapsing, it was then I saw GOD. NO...I am not saying Lillian is my 'God', what I am saying is I felt Lillian's concern for my chronic relapsing and deeper issues as a way God would deal with me. Not angry or yelling at me, not judging or telling me I am never going to get it, just that we need to work on this and find out WHY I kept relapsing.

"I can remember always wanting to be around Lillian since that day...to learn more, to see why I wanted what she had, to see someone who has gone through similar situations come as far as she did and HOW. Well today, 4 years later, maybe longer, I am. Not only am I privileged to 'hang' around her as a friend, I also now lead one of her groups at LifeCare...called Celebrate Recovery for Women! ...the same group I went to over 6 years ago."
—Carol, LifeCare volunteer

"Once I moved away to a small town where recovery groups are almost impossible to find, I realized even more what a blessing it is to have an opportunity to be among sisters who know what you are going through, understand what you feel and what it takes to restore what was or is broken. During the time I met with the recovery group, I found that I was able to freely speak about the brokenness in my heart and life and I felt no shame, no condemnation for who I was, what I was dealing with or the right way to respond. Grace seems to be the theme because you are among those who are or have been in similar situations and they desire to share that which was given to them with others. It is a blessing to know that you are not alone, that there is hope, and Christ is bigger than your pain. He led me to this group and I am ever grateful for the time and healing spent alongside other believers fighting the same battle."
—J. B., former LifeCare participant

THE CALL TO CARE

VOLUNTEER TRAINING

PART 1

For use with Volunteer Training DVD #1

OVERVIEW: GUIDING PRINCIPLES

- ***Guiding Principles for LifeCare***

1. Work within a clear and precise vision cast by the Lead
   Pastor who addresses the "human condition."

2. Volunteers and team are absolutes!

3. Understand and address the needs of your church
   attendees as well as individual and family needs in the
   community.

I. INTRODUCTION – THE CALL TO CARE

- *Biblical Foundations*

  Isaiah 61:1-3, Luke 4:18-19 and 2 Corinthians 1:3-4

  Isaiah 61:1-3
  "The Spirit of the Sovereign Lord is on me, because the Lord has anointed me to preach good news to the **poor**. He has sent me to bind up the **brokenhearted**, to proclaim freedom for the **captives** and release from darkness for the **prisoners**, to proclaim the year of the Lord's favor and the day of vengeance of our God, to **comfort all who mourn**, and provide for **those who grieve** in Zion – to bestow on them a crown of **beauty instead of ashes**, the oil of gladness instead of **mourning**, and a garment of praise instead of a spirit of **despair**. They will be **called oaks of righteousness, a planting of the Lord for the display of His splendor!**"

  Luke 4:18-19
  "'The Spirit of the Lord is on me, because he has anointed me to preach good news to the poor. He has sent me to proclaim freedom for the prisoners and recovery of sight for the blind, to release the oppressed, to proclaim the year of the Lord's favor.'"

  2 Corinthians 1:3-4
  "Praise be to the God and Father of our Lord Jesus Christ, the Father of compassion and the God of all comfort, who comforts us in all our troubles, so that we can comfort those in any trouble with the comfort we ourselves have received from God."

- ***Purpose/ Vision/ Values***

LifeCare is one way we can provide "one life at a time" opportunities for the journey to full devotion.

- ***LifeCare's Purpose & Vision***

LifeCare Christian Center is a nonprofit, inter-denominational organization providing individuals and families within the community with physical, spiritual, emotional and relational support while walking through life's challenges. It is a place where individuals and their families can share and support one another.

LifeCare Christian Center is an outreach to the entire community by providing:

- A safe place for ongoing care and support to which professionals in the fields of healthcare, law, counseling and education can refer their clients

- Care, support and recovery groups for people of all ages

- Workshops, seminars, conferences and retreats that educate participants in life skills and healthy coping mechanisms

- One-on-one care in the form of life coaching, prayer ministry and affordable counseling with contracted professionals (and trusted referrals)

- Crisis Care

- A resource center for the community – including referrals to churches that fit personality

Values that are Represented & Lived Out in LifeCare

1. _____ is the essential foundation for all effective ministry.

2. God's Word is essential to healing and the transformation of individual lives.

3. Hurting people matter to God, and therefore, matter to _____.

4. Recovery is a process by which a believer becomes _____

   _____ to Christ.

5. Continuous growth is God's will for all believers.

6. Authentic and loving relationships are developed as a result of this journey.

7. Spiritual growth, transformation and commitment happen best in

   _____   _____.

8. Excellence honors God and _____ people.

We/ The church can most visibly evidence the love of Christ by ministering to and assisting those in need with compassion and care. We have the opportunity to offer individuals and families support for their physical, emotional, and spiritual needs. We need to be "Jesus with skin on" to one another.

Truth: _____ in your church will need some form of "care" (emotional, physical, mental and/ or spiritual) at some point.

EXAMPLES

- Illness – hospital visitation/ chronic pain & illness
- Single parent family situations
- Prodigal sons/ daughters
- Death
- Benevolence
- Addictions
- Financial
- Sexual integrity
- Job loss
- Divorce
- Teen Issues – eating disorders, self-injury (cutting), pregnancy

New believers will need the opportunity to unpack the baggage they came to faith with. The baggage doesn't just "_____" when they accept Christ. It is the beginning in unloading the "stuff of their lives."

Why?

Examples:

- wrong perceptions of God
- wrong perceptions of themselves
- lies they believe
- strongholds

We have to get beyond the surface of people's lives and get into their soul (mind & emotions). We have to get into the why's of their lives—the issues beneath the surface—the matters of the heart. This is where real life change happens!

There are 3 types of people in our churches
1) those who are dealing
2) those with masks
3) those in denial

The **Iceberg is a reflection or symbol of the human condition in our churches.** The part above the water is what we see. Underneath is the reality of their lives; the stuff that is holding them back, weighing them down, and keeping them stuck and unable to move forward in their journey in becoming fully devoted followers of Jesus Christ.

Care and Support Ministries can help them deal with what is underneath.

_____

_____

_____

_____

_____

_____

_____

II. TRADITIONAL CHURCH MODELS OF CARE

The Church has traditionally presented two basic models of care:

A. **Pastoral Care** – where one or two pastors/ staff do all of the care, which is impossible! They take on benevolence applications/ interviews, hospital visits, funerals, pastoral care & counseling, etc. This kind of care is impossible to sustain, especially with growth.

Some churches have moved to providing a...

B. **Counseling Center**

There are several drawbacks to these models:
1. compassion _____/ burnout
2. spiritually gifted church members cannot participate in providing care – you are robbing them of a HUGE blessing!
3. professional counseling/ care has _____:
   - <u>financial</u> – insurance cuts
   - <u>dual relationships</u> – laws, ethical guidelines
   - <u>distant relationships</u> – alternatively, lay counselor/ caregiver relationships become up close and personal where people believe you really care and it is life impacting. Individuals realize the volunteer aspect; that

volunteers are "not paid to care", and *feel* that professionals *are* at times.

- stigma

4. cannot handle high volume of care receivers

This information helps identify and answer the next portion of our time together – Answering the "Why" question.

Why develop a system of care in the community?

_____

_____

_____

_____

_____

_____

_____

_____

_____

_____

_____

_____

_____

_____

_____

_____

III. ANSWERING THE "WHY" QUESTION

Why LifeCare?

1. What kind of people are we seeking to develop in our churches?

2. What kind of person are we looking for God to develop?

3. What does a fully devoted follower of Jesus Christ look like?

Once we have that in mind, we then need to ask ourselves...

4. What kind of person are we actually developing?

5. Are we truly seeing transformed lives?

What kind of hearts do they have? Are we seeing the "real deal" in people's lives? Are our churches places where people can be **transformed through authenticity—safe places to share what's really going on in their lives? Are we developing fully devoted followers of Jesus?**

Genuine discipleship cannot happen apart from Care (helping people deal with issues of the heart/ brokenness/ lies they believe). Individuals and families who come to us need opportunities that we can provide for healing.

_____

_____

_____

_____

People accepting Christ later in life come to Him because…

- they have needs
- they have brokenness
- they are hurting
- they need hope & healing!

LifeCare can also provide a way to provide restoration to the fallen who are in ministry. You will have a system in place to allow the opportunity for restoration to

1. God
2. the body of believers
3. ministry

I love it that many are reading and teaching from authors who write about the human condition with Biblical responses to those issues.

We have to "normalize" care in our churches. This starts with the Lead Pastor to the staff and leadership, and from the staff and leadership to the attendees.

Consider a few of Contemporary Christian Music's popular artists:

- Third Day
- Joy Williams – *Hide*
- Casting Crowns – *LifeSong* and *The Altar and the Door*

These three artists' musical works speak very much about what we are discussing today… **the human condition**… the **needs of the human soul** (mind & emotions) and how it impacts a person's spiritual life. Music/ The arts draw attention to "the elephant in the room" * – a slogan from Alcoholics Anonymous.

*☺ A condition that has existed for a very long time, that needs to be addressed, that has for far too long been ignored.

_____

_____

_____

_____

_____

THE MASK

We have the opportunity to **help individuals take their masks off, be real, heal and grow, and to not suffer in silence.** I trust that is why you are here. That you want to make a difference in people's lives like you never have before. That you want to meet their needs as Jesus has prescribed the church to do. I pray you **come on board with us and enjoy the same ride that God has us on!**

Change is happening in our churches – but it's been slow.

More and more I am hearing recovery and healing terminology coming from a variety of Christian speakers/ teachers:

- *"Get bitter or better."*
- *"We're as sick as our secrets."*
- *"If you keep doing the same thing over and over again expecting different results – that defines insanity."*

These, and more, come from Alcoholics Anonymous.

IV. SYSTEMS OF CARE (OPTION)

LifeCare's Structure/ System of Care as an Example

Who's Who on the LifeCare Team?

- o Board of Directors
- o Leadership Team
- o Teaching/ Facilitator Team
- o Volunteer & Serving Teams
- o Lay counseling/ Inner healing prayer
- o Life Coaching
- o Referrals – contracted professionals
- o Chaplains

Serving Teams:

- o Facilitators/ Teachers/ Newcomers Table
- o Hospitality
- o Library
- o Café
- o Events
- o Worship

What is Recovery/ the Support Group Experience?

Recovery is the _____, practical _____ of Biblical principles relevant to life issues. It is a journey in becoming fully devoted to Jesus Christ and experiencing the _____ He has provided for all believers.

WHAT WE ARE

- A safe place to share
- A refuge
- A place of belonging
- A place to care for others
    and be cared for
- A place where respect is given
    to each member
- A place to learn
- A place to demonstrate
    genuine love & acceptance
- A place to grow and become strong again
- A place for progress
- A place where you can take off your mask
    and allow others to really know you
- A place for healthy challenges and healthy risks
- A possible turning point in your life

WHAT WE ARE NOT

- A place for selfish control
- Group Therapy
- A place for secrets
- A place to look for dating
    relationships
- A place for perfection
- A place to judge others
- A place to "fix" others
- A quick "fix" for self

Who We Are

LifeCare is a safe place of HELP, HOPE and HEALING.

Table Talk

- How has the Support Group experience impacted your life?

- Why do you feel led to be a volunteer in this type of ministry?

What Format is Used at the "Main Event"?

- Praise & Worship: All participants join together for a time of singing and, occasionally, short praise reports.
- Announcements
- Life Application Talk or Faith Story
- Group Time

Types of Groups:
- *Processing Groups*
- *Topical Groups*
- *Low, Medium & High Risk groups*

Format of Group Time:
- Open in Prayer
- Small Group Guidelines
- Lesson
- Scripture
- Participation
- Close in Prayer

Note: Involvement in any area of the "Main Event" is always optional.

_____

_____

_____

_____

_____

What Direction is Given?

➤ Group facilitators are trained to lead small discussion groups and give direction on a limited level.

➤ In cases where the individual is dealing with deeper issues and change is difficult, individual counseling with a professional, pastor or other leader in conjunction with weekly meetings is recommended.

➤ LifeCare also has lay counselors, inner healing prayer facilitators and sponsors available to assist in an individual's healing process.

Relationship to Other Support Groups

➤ LifeCare is not formally associated with any other support group. We use methods and tools from various resources.

➤ We encourage individuals to be active in other local support, recovery, care and small groups as needed.

V. LEADERSHIP

Effective Leadership

Leadership:

- *EXPECTATIONS*
  - ➢ Complete Volunteer Training or its equivalent.
  - ➢ Attend ministry team meetings and pray for the unity, health and growth of the ministry.
  - ➢ Be faithful in attending and leading your group or performing your ministry. If unable to attend, contact the ministry team leader or co-facilitator so arrangements can be made for the group.
  - ➢ Make the Ministry Team Leader aware of any problems or "special circumstances" that arise.
  - ➢ Maintain group safety by ensuring group guidelines are followed and squelch gossip with the truth.
  - ➢ Recruit and encourage potential volunteers.
  - ➢ Participate in other training and seminar opportunities. Keep working on self and your own personal growth process.

- **BENEFITS**

    You may want to pause the DVD here and take some time as a group to brainstorm some of the benefits of serving in Care/ Support Ministries.

    _____

    _____

    _____

    _____

    _____

    _____

THE CALL TO CARE

VOLUNTEER TRAINING

PART 2, SECTION 1

For use with Volunteer Training DVD # 2

Qualities of Effective Leadership

- **GROUP WORK — BRAINSTORMING**

_____

_____

_____

_____

_____

_____

_____

_____

_____

_____

_____

_____

_____

_____

_____

_____

_____

_____

The Apostle Paul's Style of Ministry

Acts 20:17-38

- It was a ministry of _____ as well as _____.
- It was a ministry in _____ as well as _____.
- It was a ministry of _____ and _____.
- It was a ministry to _____ at _____, declaring the counsel of God.
- It was a ministry of _____, not _____.

Qualities of an Effective Leader/ Facilitator

- _____ _____: Above reproach to God – keep each other above reproach – glorify God – trustworthy – will earn the confidence and trust of others – integrity

- _____: Willing to learn from those who won't – live life to serve the best interests of others – know who they are in relation to who God is

- _____ _____: Condition of the heart is right – do not minister in bitterness – continually examine heart attitudes before God and allow him to change them

- _____ and _____: (Webster's) balance – "to regulate different powers so as to keep them in a state of just proportion." Without proper balance, Satan can get in and spoil God's plan. Physical bodies, time spent at work, Christian service, recreation – fun, rest & relaxation, balance in finances, diet, every other area

- _____ _____ _____: " The mind of Christ" – discernment – understand submission – walk in freedom to God not bondage to men – live by principle instead of rules/ laws

- _____: The weak in the faith – keep hope alive in others when they can't do it for themselves – facilitate development in others through servant hood – encourage – don't confront the newcomer or those with whom trust has not been established

Galatians 1:10

"Am I now trying to win the approval of men, or of God? Or am I trying to please men? If I were still trying to please men, I would not be a servant of Christ."

Matthew 12:20

"'A bruised reed he will not break, and a smoldering wick he will not snuff out, till he leads justice to victory.'"

Listen to this story

What do you remember?

1.

2.

3.

4.

5.

6.

7.

Active Listening Skills

Instructions: With your table group take a few moments to define and give examples of the Active Listening Skills listed.

1. **BRIEF COMMENTS**

2. **NEUTRAL PHRASES**

3. **ECHOES**

4. **OPEN-ENDED QUESTIONS**

5. **PARAPHRASING**

6. **EMPATHY STATEMENTS**

7. **SILENCE**

8. BEHAVIOR DESCRIPTION

9. GESTURES

Basic Active Listening Skills

1. Non-Verbal Attending (body language)
2. Paraphrasing (reflecting content)
3. Empathy (reflecting feeling)

Use of these three basic listening skills sends the messages:

> "I care."
>
> "I'm listening."
>
> "What you say/ feel is important."
>
> "I'll wait for you – take your time."

…and also establishes trust.

Phrases For Paraphrasing

1. "So what you're saying is _____."
2. "I hear you saying _____."
3. "If I understand you right, you're saying _____."
4. "So _____."

Phrases For Empathy

1. "It sounds like you're feeling _____."
2. "You sound _____."
3. "You look _____."
4. "You seem to be feeling _____."
5. "So, you're feeling _____."

Empathetic Listening

People recovering from loss or pain were asked, "What helps?" Their responses came down to the following:

- o Being allowed to _____ about it when I want to
- o Having all my feelings _____
- o Being with others who have had similar _____

Having patience to listen and accept what we hear is also difficult, because what we really want is to make them feel better so we can feel better. That seems more heroic.

Your goal is not to make the person "hurry through the pain," or even feel better, but to convey the fact that you care and are willing to share in the suffering. Suffering is a normal response to loss, no matter what the loss may be.

Appropriate Support

- o _____ first to see if your friend or family member would like to be with you for a while. If so, arrange for a time when the two of you can be alone.
- o Learn to be _____ with silences and with crying. If you feel you must interject, say something like, "It's hard for you to talk about it…. Just take your time" or "It's not easy to talk about this. I'll stick with you."
- o _____ with your friend or family member if it comes naturally. However, don't let your own devastation overshadow theirs. If you do that, you become the one in need of comfort, and that is not fair. It's putting your friend's need above your own.
- o Reminisce about the "good times" and continue to refer to the missing person by name if they are grieving.
- o Be especially _____ in social settings. You can be assured that many others will avoid your friend in social settings

because they won't want to face the unpleasant topic or because they don't know what to say.

Cautions

- o Don't _____ or suppress expression. Instead, encourage and enable it by asking open ended questions and giving empathetic responses without false or premature reassurance. Reassurance offered too soon can be a conversation stopper no matter how well-intended.
- o Don't be in a _____.

Listening Skills Activity

Questions, Reflections, Summarization

Instructions: Form subgroups of three and practice using questioning as a listening skill. Each member of your subgroup should take turns being the speaker, the listener (who practices the skill of questioning), and the observer.

Procedure

The speaker and listener will have a conversation of three or four minutes sharing about something they struggle with in life...work, marriage, family, children, purpose, value, etc. The observer can also time the conversation, gently announcing "stop" when the time is up.

After the conversation, take a few minutes for discussion:

First, the listener will share thoughts about how he/ she used active listening techniques. Second, the speaker will comment on his/ her experience during the conversation and the listener's use of the skills. Finally, the observer will share observations and comment on the conversation.

Next, trade roles and repeat the practice.

Each listener practice should take eight to ten minutes:

- Three or four minutes for the initial conversation and

- Three or four minutes to review it—to share the listener's and the speaker's impressions and the observer's reactions (1/2 hour).

When exchanging observations about a conversation, please give the listener accurate feedback about how he or she used the skills. If the listener is having difficulty asking open-ended questions, reflecting, or summarizing, say so and help him/ her learn how to do it better. Remember that the purpose of practice is for the listener to learn the listening skill. Feedback and suggestions from both speaker and observer are essential to the learning process.

Basic Skills for Group Leadership

- Be personally involved without relinquishing _____

- Be willing to confront in love

- Communicate _____ and _____

- Create a feeling of _____ in the group

    o Confidentiality

    o Confidence

    o Privacy

    o Boundaries

    o Christian identity

- Facilitate feedback

- Guide the _____ of anger

- Help group members connect past, present

- Help group members _____ feelings

- Integrate Biblical and psychological truth

- Operate the group on a _____ level

- Know how to start a session

- Know how to end a session

- Keep one person from dominating

- Read _____ communication

    o Posture and body orientation

    o Facial signals

    o Breathing patterns, gulps, sighs

- Utilize good listening skills

- Stay ready for _____

- Teach group members to help one another

- _____ feelings

Additional Leadership Helps

- Visiting other support groups for insights

- Dealing with problems

    o What happens if inappropriate relationships develop?

    o What if someone quits the group?

    o What if family members don't understand?

    o What if someone is not helped by the group? Some group members will gain more benefits than will others.

Qualities for Being an Effective Servant In Your Life and Your Group

Sensitivity

Be sensitive to others, where they have come from and where they are today

Colossians 3:12   Colossians 4:6   Mark 5:25-35

Encouragement

Romans 14:19   Ephesians 4:29   1 Thessalonians 5:11

Receive

Let's receive each person with love right where he/she is

Matthew 10:8   Luke 5:1-11   Mark 9:33-37

Romans 15:7   John 21:1-14

Valuable

Help each one to realize how valuable he/she is

1 John 3:1   1 Peter 2:9   John 15:16

Awareness

We need to be aware of where people are; remember them by name and their situations from week to week; be aware of special needs, those who may need extra attention and help

Colossians 1:9-11   Luke 19:1-10   Philippians 1:9

Nourishment

Our nourishment is God's Word

Romans 15:4   John 6:48-51   Psalm 119:30-31

John 6:48-51   Psalm 119:103

Time

Make time for others; extra time at a meeting, on the phone, going out for coffee, making ourselves available

1 John 3:18   Matthew 25:14-25   Luke 5:17-20

THE CALL TO CARE

VOLUNTEER TRAINING

PART 2, SECTION 2

For use with Volunteer Training DVD # 3

So You Have a Toothache? *†

	The Historian This lovable character is filled with stories of similar experiences and just can't wait to tell you all about them. *Boy, the last time I had a bad toothache, it took six weeks for them to figure out what to do. It was just awful! I went to four specialists and they finally decided I should have all my teeth pulled and wear dentures. That was about three years ago and since then I….*
	The Robber He *knows* exactly how you feel before taking time to listen to you. He literally robs you of an opportunity to speak for yourself and steals your emotion from you. *I know just how you feel! The pain and all the frustration is incredible. Your jaw hurts, your head aches, and your whole body is one giant nerve. You just want to go home.*
	Grandma Chicken Soup A first cousin to Dr. Deodorant, this advisor tries to make problems disappear with kindly actions rather than words. And the action usually starts in the kitchen. *I'm sure it's hard to chew, so why don't I run home at lunch and fix you up some nice broth to drink until you can get to the dentist? I'll make a casserole for your family and some soup for you. And I'll rent you a video, too. That way you can watch it and not think about your tooth. Here, in the meantime, just sip on this cup of hot tea. It'll make it feel all better.*
	Dr. Deodorant This "doc" can't stand unpleasantness in any form. Fortunately for you, he has the solution. Just cover up the discomfort with sweet smelling words. *You are such a nice person and do such nice things for people. It just isn't fair that you should have such an awful toothache. But I'm sure everything will turn out fine!*

The Labeler

This person seems to believe that if your problem can be categorized, labeled and pigeon-holed, everything will be just fine. The Labeler loves to use the latest buzz words and jargon.

You know what? I just bet you have Temporal Mandibular Joint Syndrome. That's what's causing your toothache. When you have TMJ, it's perfectly normal to have different teeth ache at different times. Yep! That's what you've got alright! I just know it.

Miss Bumper Sticker

Most of Miss Bumper Sticker's counsel and insight belongs on a bumper sticker. She goes through life spreading clichés and proverbs like Johnny Appleseed.

Remember, all things work together for good!

When life gives you lemons, make lemonade!

God helps those who help themselves!

After all, no pain, no gain!

The General

Here's the person who likes to give orders, directions and commands to help you straighten out the "mess" you're making out of your life.

Call the dentist right away and demand an appointment! Today!

Tell him he must see you immediately. Don't take no for an answer.

You must get that tooth taken care of without delay. Quick! Get to a phone. Call him now!

The Interrogator

This is the guy (or gal) who wants "*The facts, Ma'am. Just the facts.*" He bores in with a barrage of questions until we begin to wonder if the bright light and rubber hose are coming out next.

When did your tooth start hurting?

Which tooth is it?

Where were you when it started hurting?

Did you bite down on something hard?

How many times has this happened before?

Who's your dentist?

	The Prophet This seemingly clairvoyant advisor delights in predicting a future full of gloom and doom for you. *You know…You probably have an abscess and they'll have to either do a root canal or remove it altogether! And once they remove one, it's really hard to attach the new one to your existing teeth; but if they do, that sometimes causes your other teeth to rot. Then the whole process just starts all over again. I hate to tell you, but this could just be the beginning of your problems.*
	The Pharisee This is the perennial accuser, always ready to shake a finger at you. If you have a problem, it's your own fault. No question about it! *You should have taken better care of your teeth! Don't you realize that your body is God's temple?* *If you'd brushed and flossed regularly, you wouldn't be paying the consequences now!* *See! That's what comes from eating all those candy bars.*
	The Quick Change Artist The Quick Change Artist switches the subject smoothly, using your problem as a jumping-off point. *Speaking of dentists, my uncle is a dentist. He lives in Colorado where we vacationed last summer. You know, that was one of the best vacations we ever had. Really! The mountains are so beautiful and the hiking is great.*

* This section (character illustrations and descriptions) generously provided by
© Equipping Ministries International, Inc., 1993.
† See Alternate "Dead Dog" Scenario in Appendix.

Identifying and Dealing With Difficult People

- The key to successful relationships is responsibility!

- I am responsible for how I treat others.

- I may not be responsible for how they treat me.

- I am responsible for how I react to those who are difficult.

General Guidelines When Dealing With Difficult People

- Ask God for wisdom

- Keep healthy people in leadership

- Stay healthy yourself

- Don't give special positions to help people get better

- Be honest with God, yourself and them

- Love them

Seven Laws Of Confrontation

1. Make sure you get all the facts

2. Always confront in private

3. Never confront while you are angry

4. (When arbitrating) Always get the other person's story

5. Don't harbor a grudge

6. Listen more than you talk

7. Don't be vague about the issue, get to the point

VI. MINISTRY GOALS & TOOLS

- **Goals**

GOALS OF CARE

A. _____ : Listening, Verbal & Nonverbal Caring, Accepting

B. _____ : Hope and a Different Perspective

C. _____ : Feelings and Motives

D. _____ : Choices, Tools, Apply the steps/ curriculum/ truth, Spiritual Disciplines

E. _____ : Finding Purpose, Reaching out to others and continuing to monitor and take care of self

---

"Ministry is our love for Christ dressed up in work clothes."

"The more one takes the needs of others to heart, the more he/ she will take his/ her own heart to God."

"Be… Salt – make others thirsty for God
A Magnet – draw them closer to God
A Light – show them the way to God"

*From Navigators' *Daily Walk* devotional

SMALL DISCUSSION GROUP PROCEDURES

Preparation: Pray! Pray! Pray!

Study Curriculum Lesson and Scriptures

Bring: Bible, paper, tissues, extra pens

Be prompt in starting and ending your group

- Introduce yourself and open with prayer.

- Go over the Group Guidelines: Read, have a shared reading, or just summarize main points.

- Read key points from the lesson. Share your own experience and insights with regard to this material as a brief explanation. Feel free to use other materials available through the lending library or other approved resources.

- Open the group for discussion (**remember**: tell the participants that no one is forced to read or share – they can feel free to just listen).

- Have each participant give their name and ask them to read a Scripture and a question as part of their sharing time (Not necessary to do in this specific way; be creative and open to the Lord's leading).

- Prayer Requests: Offer to take prayer requests after each person shares, or pass around a prayer sheet at the beginning of the meeting that gives them the opportunity to write down their name and phone number (so you can call if needed). Other methods: prayer cards that are taken by each individual at the end of the group.

- Periodically invite members to get a sponsor and/ or accountability partner. Continue to encourage home study as preparation for the following week's lesson. Encourage the exchange of phone numbers for support and prayer between meetings.

- Close in prayer.

SMALL GROUP GUIDELINES DESCRIPTION

What were some of the rules/ boundaries in your family of origin? Were they clearly spelled out or did you have to guess what they were? Because of the inappropriateness or lack of rules and healthy boundaries in some of our families, it is necessary to have them in our meetings. By attending and participating in a discussion group, you are agreeing to follow the guidelines presented by the facilitator.

These rules are designed to benefit and protect individual members, the group and the leaders. Good rules create a safe atmosphere in which individual healing can occur because they offer protection, structure, and standards and they teach new ways of relating to others.

When the table facilitator is acting in his/ her role, it may be necessary for him/ her to deviate from these guidelines in order to fulfill their obligation and responsibility to the individuals at the table. The facilitator will guide and direct the members accordingly as established by this ministry and will follow through on the discernment the Holy Spirit gives him/ her. If members disagree with the conduct of the leader, they should discuss it with that leader after the meeting and, if necessary, the Ministry Team Leader and/ or Staff Pastor.

Small Group Guidelines

1. **Self-focus:** We are here to work on ourselves, not on others. We share our own experiences, insights, and feelings.

2. **Confidentiality:** What is said or done in this group is not to be discussed elsewhere (including prayer requests), except with the permission of those involved. This is absolutely necessary in order for this to be a SAFE PLACE.

3. **Respect Others:** We do not judge, criticize, analyze or "fix" others. Each of us is free to find our own answers. We encourage everyone to ask for what they need (e.g., comments/ feedback from the group, or just to be listened to).

4. **Limit Sharing:** We are considerate of the need for all to share and limit our own sharing time.

5. **Allow Feelings:** We avoid minimizing hurts, explaining them away or ignoring them. It is okay to cry and feel our emotions. Allow others to experience their feelings.

6. **Personal Space:** Have permission from the person before touching, hugging or passing tissues unless we already know it is acceptable to them to do so.

7. **Language:** This is a Christian group, so the use of offensive language is not a vehicle to be used for expression.

8. **Listen:** We will give each person our undivided attention. When feedback is requested from the group, it should be brief.

9. **Let God Work:** Members should not preach to individuals in the group.

10. **Use Discretion:** Discretion is necessary when dealing with sexual issues. Sexually explicit language should not be used in mixed groups.

CREATIVE IDEAS TO HELP YOUR GROUPS GROW AND DEVELOP

1. Pass out a prayer request sheet asking for name, phone and e-mail with their requests for you to keep at the end of the group time. Indicate that the contact information is optional. This will enable you to get their contact info for future contacts of encouragement.

2. Make a phone and e-mail list with each member's first name and have copies available at each meeting (ONLY if members agree to this).

3. At the end of the group time, have each member fill out a 3 x 5 card with a prayer request, their first name, e-mail & phone number. Trade the cards with each other and then pray for the person you get during the week and call them.

4. At the end of the group time, be sure to greet and make a special effort to talk to those who were new to the group, and get their contact information if possible.

5. Hand out small cards with Scriptures or encouraging words. These can be made or purchased at a Christian book store.

6. Plan social events for your group—do movie nights, dinner, meet for coffee.

7. Celebrate healing and growth, birthdays, anniversaries, etc. with a card, e-mail or note.

8. Call, e-mail or send a postcard to the members of your group just to let them know you are praying for them.

9. Encourage the group members to team up—pick a prayer partner/ accountability partner to call during the week. Also encourage sponsorship relationships.

10. Let your group know you are available for questions or prayer.

11. Encourage the group as a whole to be working through the curriculum, and announce upcoming study groups or seminars to enhance their journey.

12. Have a lending library for the ministry and information on area-approved Christian counselors. (Someone who represents the church or organization should be in charge of approving what literature is available.) LifeCare keeps a list available of the approved Christian Counselors where facilitators or group members can get a referral.

WHAT TO DO WHEN...

DEALING WITH PROBLEMATIC SITUATIONS

As a volunteer of LifeCare Christian Center, you are responsible for identifying and reporting life threatening problems such as suicidal or homicidal ideation, someone that is intoxicated or high on drugs, or there is suspected child abuse. Getting the support of another volunteer if at all possible to assess the situation is highly recommended. Following are situations that warrant some sort of intervention:

1. <u>Suicide</u>: Do not dismiss comments from an individual who shares about wanting to end their life, or that there is no hope. This is a cry for help. Address it directly. Talking about it openly will not make a person go out and do it; actually, the opposite is true. You may ask the individual, "Are you telling us that you are going to do something to hurt yourself? Will you make a commitment/ promise that you will not hurt yourself and that you will seek out additional support and help?" If they do not promise not to hurt themselves, do not let them leave (but do not restrain if they attempt to leave). At this point you may want to ask how they plan to hurt themselves (pills, gun, car, etc.). Then you may say, "It is not safe for you to leave. I will call someone for help." Have someone call the local emergency service (911), the police or hotline while someone stays with the individual. These are people trained to help you in such situations.

2. <u>Homicide</u>: Again, do not ignore a statement such as, "I'm going to kill them for what they did." You may ask, "Do you mean you will actually kill them, or is this a form of speech to say you wish you could?" If the individual indicates they want to actually kill someone, you may wish to find out how (gun, etc.) and as many details about the person they intend to kill (name, address, phone), and call the police immediately.

3. <u>Alcohol or Drug Intoxication</u>: The most important factor here is whether or not they intend to drive. If the person is intoxicated, steps should be taken to ensure they get home safely without driving. If you are unable to do this or they are unwilling to cooperate, call the police. If they are not driving and are not disruptive, you can allow them to stay.

4. <u>Child Abuse</u>: If an individual indicates they or another adult is sexually or physically abusing a child, discuss this immediately with your Team Leader and/ or Director who can report it to the child abuse reporting agency. It is a well-documented fact that people who abuse their children need professional intervention over an extended period of time. The child abuse agencies are equipped to investigate any suspicion of child abuse and determine the appropriate action necessary to protect the child. They can legally require the perpetrators to get the appropriate help. Do not ignore this and remember they should not be trusted to keep a promise not to hurt the child. No parent consciously wants to hurt his or her child. They cannot help themselves, so get help for them by reporting it.

5. <u>Spousal Abuse</u>: Any person who reports they are being physically or emotionally battered should be urged to seek professional help. There are battered women's shelters or hotlines for battered women. LifeCare has a list of locations and numbers. If you cannot reach someone at LifeCare, call a counseling agency or a community service agency for a referral. These shelters can provide further resources, if needed. First Step and Haven are organizations to which we frequently refer people.

In situations such as these, it is better to err on the side of more caution than to minimize a situation. It is easier to tell someone, "I over-reacted a little because I care about you" than it is to regret not having done more to save a life.

VII. PRACTICE

Small Group Scenarios (see next page)

Instructions: Role play using one or more of the Small Group Scenarios. Then, based on the Small Group Procedures and Small Group Guidelines, record your insights on what went well and what could have been better.

What Went Well?

What Could Have Been Better?

SMALL GROUP SCENARIOS

Role Play Option #1: (Pick a few experienced individuals to do this role play and others who are not experienced while the rest of the training class observes.)

Ask: course participants to observe the use of the procedures and the facilitator's skills.

Note both the successful and "needs improvement" techniques.

Facilitator Role

Facilitator opens in prayer.

Because there are new participants there is a shared reading of the Small Group Guidelines. **Note:** This is how the Guidelines will be covered for the course participants. Facilitator has the freedom to improvise, as needed. Please try to demonstrate both successful and "needs improvement" techniques as you lead the group.

Facilitator Ideas

☐ One role player doesn't want to read

☐ Facilitator agrees

☐ The lesson will be on forgiveness from Celebrate Recovery

☐ Facilitator will share concepts and begin a group discussion

☐ Role players will improvise using their situation

☐ Facilitator will tell the quiet participant, "We haven't heard much from you yet, what do you want to say?"

☐ Facilitator will put someone on the spot

☐ "How do you expect God to forgive you, if you won't forgive others?"

☐ Facilitator will ask permission to give someone a hug

☐ Facilitator will take prayer requests

☐ Facilitator will invite members to get a sponsor

☐ Facilitator will just close in prayer not acknowledging prayer requests

Participant Roles

Role: Smothering Mother/ Father

You are a person who has a son who is an alcoholic and you brought him to the meeting tonight. He's at another group, but all you can think/ talk about is how you wish he'd get sober. You are VERY concerned with his actions.

Role: Enthusiast in Denial

You are a person who loves everyone and you just know that Jesus is SO good. You continue to praise God for all the good things that are going on in your life. BUT you really are struggling with an abusive relationship that you are unable to let go of. You try to interrupt the facilitator when he or she is talking to other people at the table.

Role: Shy Guy/ Gal

You are very shy and don't like to talk. You do not want to read any of the small group guidelines when requested. You are hurting so bad inside, but you just can't bring yourself to talk about it tonight. You are new to the table.

Role: Match.comaholic

You are a person who is just fed up with life. You don't know why you've been having relationship problems. BUT your last 5 relationships were with people who somehow abused you (physically, emotionally, spiritually…pick one or all 3) and you just want to get OVER your current breakup to find Mr./Ms. RIGHT!

Role Play Option #2: (Break up into groups of 4-7 people. Pick a facilitator who will be leading the group.)

Role Play/ Practice Groups

Facilitator Role

Facilitator opens in prayer.

Because there are new participants there is a shared reading of the Small Group Guidelines. **Note:** This is how the Guidelines will be covered for the course participants. Facilitator has the freedom to improvise, as needed. Please try to demonstrate both successful and "needs improvement" techniques as you lead the group.

- **Scenario A**

Cathy finally admits that she thinks she's depressed and shows up to your Depression & Anxiety recovery group for the first time. She says she feels like she can't go on pretending any longer and wants help. She doesn't attend church very often anymore because it creates so much anxiety in her and she has a very hard time being around people lately. Admittedly, it was very hard for her to take the step of showing up at the group tonight. She tells everyone that she is having trouble sleeping and even though she makes it to work every day, it is getting more and more difficult to just get out of bed.

- **Scenario B**

This is Joe's third time at the Career Transition group. A month ago he lost his job because of downsizing at his company that he had been with for 15 years. He feels stuck and can't seem to get motivated to look for another job. His family is telling him he is irritable and they seem to be shying away from him. Your focus at the group tonight is on "dealing with loss" and how people react to it.

- **Scenario C**

Tom started coming to the group last week and this is the first time he started to open up. His wife informed him 3 weeks ago that she is filing for divorce unless he gets his anger/temper under control. Tom realizes that he has a problem with anger and has openly admitted that his father was the same way. The topic for this evening at the group is "Sources of anger and ideas on how to deal with this powerful emotion."

- **Scenario D**

Patti found out about your group from a friend who attends your church. She begins to share at the group that her husband, who is a deacon in their church, "drinks quite regularly." Sometimes when he drinks, he stays up late and then is late for work in the morning. She calls Bob's boss and tells him he is not feeling well and will be in late in hopes that this will prevent him from losing his job. There have been occasions when bob didn't make it into work at all. Patti fears that one day Bob is going to lose his job and she will have to bear the financial burden of the family. They have three children and Patti works a part time job right now.

- **Scenario E**

This is a group focused on dealing with difficulties in relationships (perhaps Conquering Codependency). The topic tonight is: Powerlessness. There are two people who are brand new to the group. One of those who is new says that they are currently with a spouse that does several things to their children that you identify as abuse. Another person at the group talks about how they are "powerless" to do anything against their spouse. There is also someone at the group that says she is not sure if she has any problems—it just seems like everyone she dates always winds up having some kind of drug problem, so she wants to learn how to pick out good guys.

As you work through this scenario, consider what the response should be to the issues brought up. What tools can you provide? Are there areas of referral that would help with any of these individuals?

- **Scenario F**

This group is a group for those making peace with their past. One person seems to be under the influence of something (drugs or alcohol). Another, who is brand new to the group, seems to have answers in response to everyone's sharing. Yet, when it comes time for him to share, he says he doesn't want to talk, he came to learn. There is another participant who is very emotional this evening, you can tell he is fighting back the tears.

As you practice this group, consider how you can protect the group members from the one with "all the answers." Are there tools from the training that you can use with any or all of these people? What are they? How would you respond to the one fighting back the feelings?

- **Scenario G**

This group is for victims of sexual abuse, and you are on the topic of forgiveness. One person is sharing very deeply, and two other members begin to have a side conversation. When another person shares, she begins to share all her pent up rage and anger and says she refuses to do this lesson.

What steps can the facilitator take to ensure everyone is respected and heard? And once you have practiced the scenario, also discuss how you handle a person who does not seem to be ready to do a particular lesson you are on for that night.

VIII. FACILITATOR REQUIREMENTS & NEXT STEPS

Next Steps for Serving as a LifeCare Small Group Leader

☐ Write Your Faith Story (see next page)

☐ Complete the Small Group Facilitator Covenant

☐ Phone or Face-to-Face Interview with LifeCare Leadership

☐ Co-Lead with an existing Facilitator

☐ Begin attending Prayer and Team Meetings

☐ _____

_____

☐ _____

_____

Personal Next Steps

Identify objectives/ things you need to do to prepare to become a Small Group Leader.

☐ _____

☐ _____

☐ _____

☐ _____

Writing Your Story

This is a guide to help you write your "faith story." God's Word tells us,

"*They overcame him (Satan)*

by the blood of the Lamb

and by the word of their testimony" *(Revelation 12:11a, NIV)*

and…

"It is a proof of your faith. Many people will praise God because you obey the Good News of Christ—the gospel you say you believe—and because you freely share with them and with all others." (2 Corinthians 9:13, NCV)

Guidelines:

- Before you start writing, pray and ask God for help.
- Be honest.
- Remember that you are not cured so sharing the fact that you have not "arrived" or that you have other challenges will not hinder your service in any way.
- Keep it short and to the point (one page if possible)
- Include a couple of your favorite Scriptures or your life verse if you have one.
- Keep in mind that this is for your leader's eyes only unless you give personal permission to use it elsewhere.

There are four major parts to your story. Relax and let's get started!

Part I: The Old You

- o What are some of the circumstances that led you to seek help and healing?
- o What was your relationship to God at that time?
- o What was your attitude toward others?

Part II: Experiences and Changes that have happened while seeking healing

- o How did I get involved with counseling/ a support group/ this healing journey?
- o How has my growing relationship with Jesus Christ influenced my healing and growth?
- o How did working through a curriculum/ study help you? (Be specific)
- o Did a specific study or person(s) touch your heart in a special way?

Part III: The New You

- o What changes has God made concerning your relationships with others?
- o What areas of your old life are gone and how has God changed you?
- o How has your walk with God changed?
- o What are some of the great benefits that you have received from seeking help?

Part IV: Reaching Out

- o What encouragement can you give someone else who is new to this journey?
- o Why do you want to be involved in care & support ministries?

NOTES

_____

_____

Icebreaker

Donald Trump	Spiderman	Samson
Bill Gates	Superman	Snow White
Oprah Winfrey	Rocky the Squirrel	Walter Cronkite
Lance Armstrong	Bullwinkle (the moose)	Underdog
George Bush	Meryl Streep	Mighty Mouse
Condolezza Rice	Sam Robertson	Sweet Polly Purebread
Katie Couric	Stone Phillips	Mother Teresa
Barbara Walters	Beyonce Knowles	Nelson Mandela
Madame Curie	Will Smith	Martin Luther King, Jr.
Princess Diana	Al Sharpton	Buddha
Minnie Mouse	Nelson Mandela	Mohammad
Mickey Mouse	Vera Wang	Osama Bin Ladin
Donald Duck	Christopher Columbus	Albert Einstein
Barney the Dinosaur	Mel Gibson	Benjamin Franklin
Dora the Explorer	Ariel Sharon	David Beckham
Miss Piggy	Prince Charles	Joe Louis
Kermit the Frog	Kanye West	Steve Yzerman
Shaquile O'Neal	Michael W. Smith	Al Kaline
Scooby Doo	Abraham Lincoln	Dolly Parton
Neil Armstrong	Dick Cheney	Joe Montana
Prince Charles	Joyce Meyer	Chauncy Billups
Camilla Parker Bowles	Franklin Graham	Rick (Rip) Hamilton
Meredith Viera	Judas Iscariot	Walt Disney
Pat Robertson	Simon Peter	Tom Hanks
Kenny Rogers	Job	Wonder Woman
Arnold Schwarzenegger	Eve	Hillary Clinton
Judge Judy	Adam	Stevie Wonder
Dr. Phil	Mary (mother of Jesus)	Diana Ross

THE JORDAN MANAGEMENT CONSULTANTS

To Jesus, Son of Joseph
Woodcrafters Carpenter's Shop
Nazareth, 25922

Dear Sir,

Thank you for submitting the resumés of the twelve men you have for management positions in your new organization. All of them have now taken our battery of tests; and we have not only run the results through our computer, but also arranged personal interviews for each of them with our psychologist and vocational aptitude consultant. The profiles of all tests are included, and you will want to study each of them carefully. As part of our advice and for your guidance, we make some general comments, much as an auditor will include some general statements. This is given as a result of staff consultation and comes without any additional fee.

It is the staff opinion that most of your nominees are lacking in background, education, and vocational aptitude for the type of enterprise you are undertaking. They do not have the team concept. We would recommend that you continue your search for persons of experience in managerial ability and proven capability. Simon Peter is emotionally unstable and given to fits of temper. Andrew has absolutely no qualities of leadership. The two brothers, James and John, the sons of Zebedee, place personal interest above company loyalty. Thomas demonstrates a questioning attitude that would tend to undermine morale. We feel that it is our duty to tell you that Matthew has been blacklisted by the Greater Jerusalem Better Business Bureau. James, the son of Alpheus, and Thaddeus definitely have radical leanings. One of the candidates, however, shows great potential. He is a man of ability and resourcefulness, ambitious, and responsible. We recommend Judas Iscariot as your controller and right-hand man. All of the other profiles are self-explanatory.

Sincerely Yours,
Jordan Management Consultants
Jerusalem 26544 (Copied from Pulpit Helps)

Aren't you glad Jesus was making the decisions?

*"The Mask"**

Don't be fooled by me. Don't be fooled by the face I wear; for I wear a mask—a thousand masks; masks that I'm afraid to take off, and none of them are really me. Pretending is an art that's second nature to me, but don't be fooled.

I give you the impression that I'm secure, that all is sunny and unruffled with me, within as well as without. Confidence is my name and coolness is my game. I am in command. I need no one. But don't believe me—please. My surface may seem smooth but my surface is my mask, my ever-changing and ever-concealing mask. Beneath dwells the real me in confusion, in fear, in aloneness. But I hide this. I don't want anybody to know it.

I panic at the thought of my fear and weakness being exposed. That's why I frantically create a mask to hide behind, a nonchalant, sophisticated facade—to help me pretend; to shield me.

Acceptance, followed by love is what I need. It is one thing that will assure me that I'm really worth something. But I don't tell you this. I don't dare. I'm afraid to. I'm afraid that you'll think less of me, that you'll laugh, and your laugh would kill me.

My life becomes a front. I idly chatter to you in the suave tones of surface talk. I tell you everything that's really nothing, and nothing of what's everything. So when I'm going through my routine, do not be fooled by what I'm saying. Please listen carefully and try to hear what I'm not saying, what I'd like to be able to say, but what I'm afraid to say.

I dislike the superficial game I'm playing—the superficial, phony game. I'd really like to be genuine and spontaneous and me. But that fear—that wall of fear…it stops me every time. My survival depends on breaking through that wall. It depends on me…fighting my fear, shedding my mask and showing myself to you. But I am scared. I'm afraid that deep down I'm nothing—that I'm just no good, and that you'll see this and reject me.

So, I play my game, my desperate, pretending game, with a facade of assurance without, and a trembling child within, and so begins the parade of masks.

—Author Unknown

*Modified from original version

FAITH

The fields were parched and brown from lack of rain, and the crops lay wilting from thirst. People were anxious and irritable as they searched the sky for any sign of relief. Days turned into arid weeks. No rain came.

The ministers of the local churches called for an hour of prayer on the town square the following Saturday. They requested that everyone bring an object of faith for inspiration.

At high noon on the appointed Saturday the townspeople turned out en masse, filling the square with anxious faces and hopeful hearts. The ministers were touched to see the variety of objects clutched in prayerful hands—holy books, crosses, rosaries.

When the hour ended, as if on magical command, a soft rain began to fall. Cheers swept the crowd as they held their treasured objects high in gratitude and praise. From the middle of the crowd one faith symbol seemed to overshadow all the others: A small nine-year-old child had brought an umbrella.

Alternate "Dead Dog" Scenario

Adverse Advisors Script – Option #2: My Dog Died (This scenario could be used in place of the Toothache scenario, at the end of Section V, in helping your group leaders to understand the various personalities that they will encounter in their groups.)

Seeker: Gee, I feel terrible. My dog was killed by a car last week and the whole family is depressed.

The Interrogator: When did it happen?

How did you first hear of the accident?

Did he live long?

Who was driving the car?

Was he speeding?

Was the dog insured?

How long had you had the dog?

The General: Now you'll feel better if you go to the dog pound right now and get another dog. You need to forget that other dog; quit thinking of the past and focus on the future.

The Pharisee: Well, you have to be more careful what you let your dog do. You know it's not very smart to let a dog run around on the streets.

The Labeler: You're simply a victim of the grief process. Being in grief you can expect to feel this way. It's perfectly normal to have grief, even over a dog.

Grandma Chicken Soup: Why don't I have you and the kids over for a big party. I'll fix ice cream and cake for dessert, and we can watch "Ole Yeller" on T.V.

The Historian: I lost a dog once. Broke my heart. Never got over it either. I was only 10 when it happened.

Miss Bumper Sticker: Here today, gone tomorrow.

Life goes on.

No pain, no gain.

Into every life a little rain must fall.

Well, I've got to go. Time is money. See you in church.

Confidential Class/Group Evaluation

1. Is this group/class contributing to your growth and progress in this area? If yes, how? If not, why not?

2. Is the material easy to understand? Should it be more in-depth? If so, in what sections?

3. What do you like most about the class?

4. What do you like least about the class and/or what would you like to change?

5. Are there particular questions that you have about the topic that you would like to see discussed in future classes? If so, please share.

6. Given the following options, select the statements that apply to this class/group (please circle all that apply). I would prefer...

   - More group discussion
   - More examples
   - Less examples
   - More structure/follow curriculum
   - More deviation of workbook material – you did the homework, you don't want to go over it in class.
   - Question and answers at the end of class
   - Questions throughout the class

7. Additional comments:

FACILITATOR COVENANT

As a small group facilitator, I agree and commit to the following:

1. I have received Jesus Christ as my Savior and am committed to live my life for Him.

2. I will strive to live an exemplary life, following the teachings laid before me in the Scriptures (i.e., the Ten Commandments, the Beatitudes, the book of Romans, etc.). In order to do this, I am committed to pray, study the Scriptures and continue to grow in my knowledge of healing and growth.

3. I realize that, in a leadership role, I will be guiding hearts and minds toward our Lord, healing, recovery and maturity. In order to do this, I also understand that I must be sound and stable mentally, emotionally and spiritually. Should changes occur in my life and I feel I cannot live up to these commitments, I will inform the Ministry Team Leader and/ or the Care Ministries Pastor and temporarily step down from my position.

4. I have been working my own healing and growth for at least one year or the equivalent and have victory in my life.

5. I sense the Lord's calling and His empowerment to be a small group facilitator and servant in this ministry.

6. I am willing to attend future conferences, seminars and meetings when offered for training in the area of leadership and issues pertaining to my area of ministry.

7. I have read the vision, purpose and values of this ministry and have a clear understanding of what my responsibilities are to my church, this ministry and to the Lord.

8. I am submitting myself to the guidance and leadership of this ministry/ my church and understand my responsibilities as such.

_____
Signature

_____
Date

LifeCare Statement of Faith - What We Believe

...*a safe place of help, hope & healing*

We believe that the Bible is the inspired Word of God, inerrant in its original manuscripts. The Bible is our supreme and final authority in faith and life. (2 Timothy 3:16; 2 Peter 1:20-21)

We believe in one God, eternally existing in three Persons: Father, Son and Holy Spirit, each of whom possesses equally all the attributes of deity and the characteristics of personality. We believe that in the beginning God created out of nothing the world and all the things therein, thus manifesting the glory of His power, wisdom and goodness. By His sovereign power, He continues to sustain His creation. By His providence, He is operating throughout history to fulfill His redemptive purposes. (Genesis 1:1, 26; Matthew 28:19; John 1:1, 3; 4:24; Acts 5:3-4; Romans 1:20; Ephesians 4:5-6; 2 Corinthians 13:14)

We believe that Jesus Christ was conceived by the Holy Spirit, born of the Virgin Mary and is true God and true man. (Matthew 1:18-25; Luke 1:25-38; Romans 9:5; Titus 2:13)

We believe that man was created in the image of God, that he sinned and thereby incurred not only physical death, but also spiritual death which is separation from God, and that all human beings are born with a sinful nature, and become guilty sinners in thought, word and deed. (Genesis 1:26-27; 3:1-24; Romans 3:25; 5:12-18; I John 1:8)

We believe that the Lord Jesus Christ died for our sins according to the Scriptures as a representative and substitutionary sacrifice; that He rose victorious from the grave on the third day; and that all who believe in Him are justified on the grounds of His shed blood. (Isaiah 53; Matthew 20:28; John 3:16; Romans 3:24-26; 5:1; I Corinthians 15:3; 2 Corinthians 5:21; Ephesians 1:7; I John 2:2; Matthew 28:6; Romans 10:9; I Corinthians 15:14)

We believe that we can have a personal relationship with God through salvation, God's free gift to man. It is not a result of what we do, but it is only available through God's unearned favor. By admitting we have sinned and believing in the death, burial and resurrection of Christ, and accepting Him as Lord, we can spend eternity with God. (Ephesians 2:8-9 ; Romans 5:1 ; Romans 3:24)

We believe that all who come by grace through repentance and faith to accept the Lord Jesus Christ are born again of the Holy Spirit and thereby become children of God. (John 1:12-13; 3:3, 5; James 1:18; I Peter 1:23; Ephesians 2:8-9)

We believe that the Holy Spirit, the third Person of the Trinity, was sent into the world by the Father and the Son to apply to mankind the saving work of Christ. We believe that He enlightens the minds of sinners, awakens in them recognition of their need for a Savior and regenerates them.

We believe that, at the point of salvation, He permanently indwells every believer to become the source of assurance, strength, and wisdom, and uniquely endows each believer with gifts for ministry. We believe that the Holy Spirit guides believers in understanding and applying the Scripture. We believe that His power and control are appropriated by faith, making it possible for the believer to lead a life of Christ-like character and to bear fruit to the glory of the Father. (John 14:16-17, 26; 15:26-27; 16:8-11, 13; Romans 8:9; 1 Corinthians 2:9-14; 6:19-20; Hebrews 9:14)

LifeCare Statement of Faith

We believe God has given each person gifts to be used for the good of Christ's kingdom. We believe Christians are to develop and exercise their God-given gifts in church, the world, and at home. All believers, without regard to gender, ethnicity, and class, are free and encouraged to use their God-given gifts in ministries, communities, and families. (Galatians 3:28; 1 Corinthians 7:3-6; 11:11-12; Galatians 6:2; Ephesians 4:16)

We believe God is <u>Love</u> and He loves all people. It is His desire to reach out to those who are poor, oppressed, widowed, or orphaned and to heal the brokenhearted. (Psalm 68:5-6; 1 John 4:16)

We believe divine healing is active in the lives of people today through Jesus, who is the Healer. Healing includes physical, mental, emotional and spiritual restoration. (Luke 9:11; Matthew 9:35; Acts 10:38; Matthew 10:1)

We believe in the personal and imminent return of our Lord Jesus Christ. (Acts 1:11; I Thessalonians 4:16-17)

We believe in the bodily resurrection of the just and the unjust, the everlasting joy of the saved and the everlasting conscious punishment of the lost. (John 5:28-29; I Corinthians 15; 2 Corinthians 5:10; Matthew 25:31-46; Revelation 20:4-6, 11-15)

We believe that water baptism is the Biblical testimony of the professed believer in the name of the Father, Son and Holy Spirit. (Acts 2:28-41, 47; Matthew 28:18-20; Acts 8:36-40; 10:47; 18:8; Romans 6:3-4; I Corinthians 12:13)

We believe that those who partake of the Lord's Supper should be born-again believers, walking in fellowship with the Lord Jesus Christ. (Acts 2:42-46; I Corinthians 11:23-29)

We believe that there is one true Church universal, comprised of all those who acknowledge Jesus Christ as Lord and Savior. We believe that the Scripture commands believers to gather together to devote themselves to worship, prayer, the teaching of the Word, the observance of believers baptism and communion as the ordinances established by Jesus Christ, fellowship, service to the body through the development and use of talents and gifts and outreach to the world. We believe that wherever God's people meet regularly in obedience to this command, there is the local expression of the Church, and its members are to work together in love and unity, intent on the one ultimate purpose of glorifying Christ. (Hebrews 10:24-25; Acts 2:42-47)

Fill-in-the-Blank Answers

I. Introduction – The Call to Care

Values that are Represented & Lived Out in LifeCare

1. _____PRAYER_____ is the essential foundation for all effective ministry.
2. God's Word is essential to healing and the transformation of individual lives.
3. Hurting people matter to God, and therefore, matter to _____US_____.
4. Recovery is a process by which a believer becomes _____FULLY_____ _____DEVOTED_____ to Christ.
5. Continuous growth is God's will for all believers.
6. Authentic and loving relationships are developed as a result of this journey.
7. Spiritual growth, transformation and commitment happen best in _____SMALL_____ _____GROUPS_____.
8. Excellence honors God and _____INSPIRES_____ people.

Truth: _____**Everyone**_____ in your church will need some form of "care" (emotional, physical, mental and/ or spiritual) at some point.

New believers will need the opportunity to unpack the baggage they came to faith with. The baggage doesn't just _" disappear "_ when they accept Christ. It is the beginning in unloading the "stuff of their lives."

II. Traditional Church Models of Care

There are several drawbacks to these models:

1. compassion <u>fatigue</u>/ burnout
2. spiritually gifted church members cannot participate in providing care – you are robbing them of a HUGE blessing!
3. professional counseling/ care has <u>limitations</u>:

IV. Systems of Care (Option)

What is Recovery/ the Support Group Experience?

Recovery is the ___progressive___, practical ___application___ of Biblical principles relevant to life issues. It is a journey in becoming fully devoted to Jesus Christ and experiencing the ___fulfillment___ He has provided for all believers.

V. Leadership

The Apostle Paul's Style of Ministry

Acts 20:17-38

- It was a ministry of ___transparency___ as well as ___teaching___.
- It was a ministry in ___public___ as well as ___private___.
- It was a ministry of ___tears___ and ___triumphs___.
- It was a ministry to ___all people___ at ___all times___, declaring the counsel of God.
- It was a ministry of ___selflessness___, not ___selfishness___.

Qualities of an Effective Leader/ Facilitator

- ___Disciplined___ ___Life___: Above reproach to God – keep each other above reproach – glorify God – trustworthy – will earn the confidence and trust of others – integrity

- ___Humility___: Willing to learn from those who won't – live life to serve the best interests of others – know who they are in relation to who God is

- ___Pure___ ___Motives___: Condition of the heart is right – do not minister in bitterness – continually examine heart attitudes before God and allow him to change them

- ___Stability___ and ___Balance___: (Webster's) balance – "to regulate different powers so as to keep them in a state of just proportion." Without proper balance, Satan can get in and spoil God's plan. Physical bodies, time spent at work, Christian service, recreation – fun, rest & relaxation, balance in finances, diet, every other area

- ___Becoming___ ___More___ ___Mature___: "The mind of Christ" – discernment – understand submission – walk in freedom to God not bondage to men – live by principle instead of rules/ laws

- _____Acceptance_____: The weak in the faith – keep hope alive in others when they can't do it for themselves – facilitate development in others through servant hood – encourage – don't confront the newcomer or those with whom trust has not been established

Empathetic Listening

People recovering from loss or pain were asked, "What helps?" Their responses came down to the following:

- Being allowed to <u>talk</u> about it when I want to
- Having all my feelings <u>accepted</u>
- Being with others who have had similar <u>experiences</u>

Appropriate Support

- ___Call___ first

- Learn to be <u>comfortable</u> with silences and with crying

- <u>Cry</u> with your friend or family member if it comes naturally

- Reminisce about the "good times" and continue to refer to the missing person by name if they are grieving

- Be especially <u>attentive</u> in social settings

Cautions

- o Don't <u>force</u> or suppress expression
- o Don't be in a <u>hurry</u>

<u>Basic Skills for Group Leadership</u>

- Be personally involved without relinquishing <u>leadership</u>

- Be willing to confront in love

- Communicate <u>acceptance</u> and <u>concern</u>

- Create a feeling of <u>safety</u> in the group

- Facilitate feedback

- Guide the <u>expressions</u> of anger

- Help group members connect past, present

- Help group members <u>identify</u> feelings

- Integrate Biblical and psychological truth

- Operate the group on a <u>feeling</u> level

- Know how to start a session

- Know how to end a session

- Keep one person from dominating

- Read <u>non-verbal</u> communication

- Utilize good listening skills

- Stay ready for <u>anything</u>

- Teach group members to help one another

- <u>Validate</u> feelings

VI. Ministry Goals & Tools

GOALS OF CARE

A. _____COMFORT_____ : Listening, Verbal & Nonverbal

Caring, Accepting

B. _____ENCOURAGEMENT_____ : Hope and a Different Perspective

C. IDENTIFICATION / VALIDATION : Feelings and Motives

D. _____GROWTH_____ : Choices, Tools, Apply the

steps/ curriculum/ truth, Spiritual

Disciplines

E. _____MATURITY_____ : Finding Purpose, Reaching out to

others and continuing to monitor and

take care of self

RECOMMENDED READING

The Emotionally Healthy Church – Peter Scazzero with Warren Bird

Emotionally Healthy Spirituality: Unleash the Power of Authentic Life in Christ –

    Peter Scazzero

The Disciple Making Church: From Dry Bones to Spiritual Vitality – Glenn

    McDonald

Living Beyond the Sanctuary – Glenn McDonald

Everyone's Normal Till You Get to Know Them – John Ortberg

Waking the Dead – John Eldredge

UNChristian – David Kinnaman

Caring Enough to Confront – David W. Augsburger

RECOMMENDED ORGANIZATIONS, CURRICULUM &

RESOURCES

LifeCare Publishing: available at www.lifecarechristiancenter.org

Saddleback Church – Celebrate Recovery: www.celebraterecovery.com

American Association of Christian Counselors: www.aacc.net

Christians in Recovery: http://christians-in-recovery.org

ABOUT THE AUTHOR

LILLIAN M. EASTERLY-SMITH, B.C.P.C.

Lillian M. Easterly-Smith is the Founder, Executive Director and Community Care Pastor of LifeCare Christian Center. Lillian's experience spans over 25 years, beginning as a volunteer for Alcoholics for Christ (AC). She served on their board of directors, led support & recovery groups, led worship, organized retreats, and taught in many workshops, seminars and classes. Lillian, along with a volunteer team, developed the curriculum for Adult Children of Dysfunctional Families, which was adopted by AC as one of their core curriculums.

Lillian has served as speaker, teacher and leader of pilot programs, ministries and support groups for victims of various forms of abuse, addictions, and dysfunctional family issues as well as counseled individuals and couples. She has volunteered and been employed at two major churches where she oversaw the development of care, support & recovery group ministries which grew from three groups and 12 volunteers, to over 60 groups with approximately 500 attendees each week and included a vibrant lay counseling ministry. Lillian managed a paid staff of nine and a volunteer staff of approximately 300. She holds a degree in Counseling/Psychology and Biblical Studies; is a Licensed Pastor; Licensed,

Ordained Chaplain with I.F.O.C. (International Fellowship of Chaplains) and a Board Certified Pastoral Counselor through the International Board of Christian Counselors (American Association of Christian Counselors).

Lillian Easterly-Smith is sought after as a speaker and workshop leader for caregivers, counselors and pastors. Her extensive qualifications and unique God-given gifts have equipped her to affect change in the lives of hundreds, if not thousands, of people. She has trained hundreds of volunteers over the years and helped many churches develop care ministries that offer care, support & recovery groups.

Lillian resides in Southeast Michigan with her husband, Mike Smith. She has an adult daughter and two beautiful grandchildren.

ABOUT THE CO-PRESENTER

PATTI RADZIK

Patti Radzik was a member of the LifeCare Christian Center board of directors for four years. She has 22 years' experience in the non-profit event management field, and currently serves as director of corporate partnerships for the National Multiple Sclerosis Society, Michigan Chapter. Her passion is for the lost, hurting, and the least of these; to help others find hope in the grace of Jesus Christ; to "act justly and to love mercy and to walk humbly with God" (Micah 6:8). Her dream is to love and breathe life into the orphans in Swaziland, Africa and to see God raise them up to be disciples and world changers.

TRAINING EVALUATION/ FEEDBACK

1. What did you like most about the training?

_____

_____

_____

_____

2. What did you like least about the training?

_____

_____

_____

_____

3. What suggestions would you give to improve the training?

_____

_____

_____

_____

4. Are there any areas in which you would like additional training?

_____

_____

_____

_____

5. Any additional comments, questions or suggestions?

_____

_____

_____

_____

_____